Shine from
Within

Shine from Within

ISBN 9798612460787 paperback

For the one who has always believed in my light

Contents

The Light Within

You shine so bright, as you are right now,
flaws and faults entirely.

Made of light

You are made of the brightest stars and the widest oceans. You are made of the same things as the highest mountains and the tallest trees. Your eyes shine of sunshine and your heart glows of light. You come from heroes and warriors, kings and queens. You have gods and goddesses flowing through your veins. Beautiful friend, you are made of the universe itself. You are made of magic and light, dreams and wishes. If you've ever doubted it, if anyone has ever tried to convince you of otherwise, know that you shine so bright, as you are right now, flaws and faults entirely.

Made for light

Your heart is meant to be full of love and your belly is supposed to ache from laughter. Your eyes are meant to crinkle on the edges from smiling so much and your soul is meant to feel joy with each new day you are gifted. You are meant to feel peace when you rise each morning and again when you lie your head down to rest each night. Beautiful friend, *this* is what your natural state is. *This* is what light feels like... Peace. Excitement. Love. Joy. Laughter. Happiness. Gratitude... *This* is what you are made of and what you are made for.

Within

When you feel like you are surrounded by darkness, remember that you hold endless light within your own beating heart. Remember that you hold this light even when it feels like your world is falling apart, even when you feel like you can't keep it all together for another moment. Look for it within you. I promise that it's there. There is still boundless hope in your heart. There is still beautiful peace within. There is still incredible light in your soul. You will feel light again and you will feel peace again. No darkness out there could *ever* compete with the light you hold within.

Light always wins

No matter how long you've been facing the dark, no matter how endless it may feel, know that your light is coming. Know that no darkness ever lasts. The darkest nights *always* end in dawn. The darkest storms *always* end in peaceful light. A single flame can light even the darkest room. A single star can shine out the darkness of the night... Look for that light no matter how difficult it is. Look for the small flame, look for the single star because soon, that flame won't be small and that star won't be alone. Soon, your world will be full of shining light.

You are worth more than gold even
when you have nothing.

Self worth

The only one who can decide your worth is you. And that's the thing; you must *decide* your worth. You must decide that you're worthy of your own love and compassion. You must decide that you're worthy of feeling joy. You must decide that you're worthy of feeling happiness and peace and love and light... No matter if you've thought differently before, no matter if anyone has tried to convince you of otherwise, beautiful friend, your worth comes from *you*.

You are worthy

You don't need to have a certain amount of money before being worthy of joy, of love. You don't need to have a certain job or status, a certain number of friends. You don't need to have any amount of notifications or messages. You don't need to prove yourself to be worthy because true worth comes from within. It will never come from a number out there— not a dollar amount, not a number of notifications nor a gpa. It won't come from the number of nights you spend out or the number of days you spend on vacation. What's often forgotten is that those numbers will change with time, but what won't change is who you are deep inside: limitless, strong, brave, beautiful, courageous, creative, wonderful; and *that's* what makes you worthy.

More than gold

You are worth more than gold even when you have nothing. You are worthy of feeling joy even after you've made a mistake. You are worthy of feeling happy even when you don't have everything figured out. You are worthy of your own kindness even when others are unkind to you. Beautiful friend, always remember that you are worth more than gold. You are worthy right now, exactly as you are today as you read these words. You are worth everything.

Prove

You don't need to prove anything. You don't need to prove that you can handle it all. You don't need to prove that you are strong enough or brave enough or smart enough. You don't need to prove that you are better off or worse off than anyone else. You don't need to justify yourself or your every action… You are allowed to simply be. You are allowed to be yourself and do what you think is right, without needing to justify it. You are human, you are worthy.

Roots

It doesn't matter if you come from a small home or a large home. It doesn't matter if you come from a large family or if you never knew your parents. It doesn't matter if you are 18, 38, 58, or 88 years old. It doesn't matter if you had a 1.9 gpa or a 4.0 gpa in high school. It doesn't matter if you never finished high school or if you graduated from a large university. It doesn't matter if you come from out in the country or from the city lights. It just doesn't matter. Deep inside, every single person— *every. single. person*— is worthy of joy, and not just worthy, but *meant for* joy. No matter where you come from, no matter what you've been through, no matter what darkness you've seen, you are worthy of joy.

You are worthy of joy
regardless of your circumstances.

Joy

Joy doesn't care where you are from. Joy doesn't just visit big homes or little homes. Smiles don't just come to those who work in local shops or large corporate offices. Laughter doesn't care if you have all of your teeth or if you're missing ten. Peace doesn't care if you're meditating in the mountains or relaxed watching your favorite show. You are human. You are worthy of joy regardless of your circumstances. You are worthy of peace regardless of what you've been through. You are worthy of laughter regardless of the darkness you've faced.

Listen

Listen to the little voice inside of you that knows you are beautiful, that knows you are made of magic and gold. The voice that whispers *yes, you can*, even when those around you say you can't. It's the voice that believes it's possible even before there is any evidence of it working out. It's the voice that says *you are so beautiful* with or without makeup on, and regardless of if you're wearing your sweats or your finest dress. This is your voice of truth, your voice of worth, your voice of power. You've listened to the voice of doubt and fear before. You've listened to the voice that says you're not worthy. But that voice never gave you joy. That voice never fed you truth. That voice *only* hindered you. So maybe it's time to start listening to the one that knows you are meant for so much more.

You are not ordinary.
Beautiful friend, you are immeasurable.

Extraordinary

Beautiful friend, you are not ordinary; you never have been. You are *extraordinary*. You are beautiful in so many more ways than you can imagine. You are more interesting than you could ever understand. You are incredibly unique in how you see and interact with the world around you. You hold dreams and ideas inside of you that no one else has ever thought of, and that the world so desperately needs. You make a huge difference in those around you. Your smiles brighten days. Your hugs heal wounds... Never forget that you are extraordinary.

Immeasurable

Maybe you did have an "average" gpa. Maybe you make an "average" amount of money. Maybe you have an "average" home. But you and everything that encompasses you is *extraordinary*. Dreams don't have numbers. Ideas aren't measured. The depth of your heart and soul cannot be put into words. The value of your love and kindness cannot truly be expressed. So maybe some things about your life are expressed as average numbers. That's okay. Because your soul isn't ordinary. Your heart isn't ordinary. Your mind isn't ordinary. Your impact on the world around you is extraordinary. Beautiful friend, you are immeasurable.

The heart knows

Where did your doubts come from? Who planted those seeds of fear inside of you? When did you start believing you were anything less extraordinary? Who told you that you couldn't? Beautiful friend, I promise that those doubts and fears didn't come from your own heart. They came from someplace out there. They came from that teacher who didn't really see you or that coach who didn't believe in you. They came from that bully or that envious friend… Your heart knows you are made for more though. Your heart knows you are incredibly wonderful in so many ways. Your heart knows you are worthy. Maybe it's time to start listening to your heart and believing in you too.

Seeds

Every belief you have about yourself started as just one little seed in your mind. A parent who always believed in you gave you a seed of encouragement. A friend who always said you were so strong and beautiful gave you a seed of confidence… But a coach who always sat you out gave you a seed of doubt. A bully who always made fun of you gave you a seed of worthlessness… So, it's time to look at your garden. It's time to rip out those weeds no matter how long they've been there and plant some new seeds in their place. It's time to plant your own seeds of love and encouragement, hope and faith. It's time to nourish your flowers of confidence, of worth, of potential. Keep watering and giving light to those flowers. Keep pulling out the weeds. Give your attention only to what you want to see grow.

Enough

You are good enough. You are strong enough. You are smart enough. Stop thinking otherwise. Other people may put you down, other people may not see your worth. But *you* must always believe in your worth. You aren't meant to carry these fears and doubts with you. You aren't meant to hold others' criticisms within your own heart. Believe in who you are because you are truly lovely, and you *are* good enough. You are strong and smart enough. You are so much more than you can imagine. You are so much more than enough.

Stars

Like a beautiful star shining in the night sky, your purpose is not to compare your light or brightness to any other star. Your purpose is not to wish you were a moon or a planet, or to wish you were somewhere else. Your purpose is not to change who you are or what you are made of. Your purpose is to shine your light as bright and as beautiful as only you can. Your purpose is to celebrate the light of others while celebrating your own light too. Because it is only when we are all shining our own unique lights can we light up the entire night sky.

Nourish Your Flame

Remind yourself that wherever you are
in your journey right now,
you're exactly where you're supposed to be.

Pause

Pause… Amidst the busyness. During the days of back to back appointments, celebrations and meetings. During the moments when life seems to be moving at one hundred miles per hour. Pause… Take it all in, right where you are now. Reacquaint yourself with who you are. Remind yourself that you are doing your best and that that is enough. Pause… Allow your muscles to take a moment to stretch and feel them release their tension. Pause… Take in as much air as your lungs will allow and just breathe.

Slow

S...l...o...w... it all down. Take a break from your full calendar for a moment—or ten— to simply be. To remind yourself that this is life, right here, right now, and that this life really is beautiful. Slow down from the world spinning around you to simply wiggle your fingers and toes. To remember that life is precious and fragile and should be lived in joy. Slow it down every now and again to remind yourself that whatever is happening or wherever you may find yourself in your journey right now, it's all as it's supposed to be.

Notice

Don't let your life go by unnoticed. Life is made of moments full of beauty and magic, waiting for us to notice them. You must not let the distractions and busyness keep you from experiencing everything this beautiful life has to offer. Notice how the colors of the sun rise each morning. Take an extra moment to appreciate the new flowers in bloom. Notice the way your friend's eyes light up when they're talking about their day. Enjoy the last sip of your morning coffee as much as you did the first one. Savor those moments of putting your head down on your pillow after a long day. Notice the little moments because someday, you'll realize they were never really that little after all.

Intentional

Watch the sunset with the only intention of watching the sun gloriously set into the night. Look at your partner's face deeply and tenderly, with the only intention of truly seeing them. Eat dinner without rush to savor the meal and the time with your loved ones. Rest without distraction to let yourself completely unwind… Regardless of where you are or what you are doing, allow yourself to be entirely there.

Later will come,
but right now you are here.
And here is wonderful.

Now

When you find your mind drifting into worries about tomorrow, worries about that big day coming up, return to the beautiful moment of now, where everything is exactly as it should be. I know it's incredibly hard sometimes, and I know you can't help but let your mind think about later… But don't let those thoughts keep you from enjoying the beautiful moment you are in right now. Know that later will come when it's time, but right now you are here. And here is wonderful too.

Breathe

When you are feeling overwhelmed, allow yourself to create moments to simply be. To notice how you are really feeling and if you are tense. To notice your breathing and how rapidly or slowly your lungs are working. Allow yourself moments of peace, moments to notice, moments to feel, moments to *simply breathe*.

Rest

You don't always have to be doing something.
You *are* allowed to slow down; you are allowed to take breaks from your never-ending lists and on-going tasks. You are allowed to take breaks to simply be with yourself and your own thoughts. You can slow down, you are allowed to rest. In fact, you *must* make time for yourself. You must take time to consume nothing but the little world around you wherever you are. Take time to give your soul breaks. Take time for you, beautiful friend. Take time for you.

Checklists

Don't worry if you didn't check off every task today. Don't worry if your to-do list is massive and feels like it's only growing larger. Don't worry if you feel like you didn't make any progress today. Life isn't just about checking boxes or crossing off lists. It's about giving what you can each day and then *moving on*. Some days you won't be able to give anything, and that's okay. Every day is not the same and every day is not meant to be the same. You aren't a machine built to check off lists. You're a real person, with real feelings and a real soul. You need rest. You deserve peace. Because if you're giving what you can, you're giving everything. And that really is enough.

The wonderful

You don't have to have it all together. Beautiful friend, you don't even have to have it somewhat together. Sometimes things fall apart. Sometimes our plans don't work out in the slightest. Sometimes life throws so many curveballs at once that all we can do is try our best to hold on. So it's time to let go of all the images of how you thought it was supposed to be because the truth is that nobody's life is perfect. No one has it all figured out. Life throws *everyone* curveballs. Life gets messy for us all sometimes. Your life was never meant to be perfect anyhow; your life is meant to be real. You are made to have some messiness because that's how you make time for the wonderful.

Let yourself shine. Let your smile light up the room.
Let your excitement spread to those around you.

Feelings

Be gentle with yourself, beautiful friend. Let yourself feel everything you need to feel. When you're sad, allow yourself to cry it out. When you're frustrated, allow yourself to get good and frustrated and get it all out of your system. When you're really bothered, figure out why it's bothering you so much and then find it in your heart to let it go. And when you're happy, oh beautiful friend, when you're happy, let yourself shine. Let your smile light up the room. Let your excitement spread to those around you. Let your laughter bring a ray of sunshine.

Even when you think you are supposed
to be strong, it's okay not to be.

It's okay

It's okay to feel down. It' s okay to not hold it all together. It's okay to wish things were different. Beautiful friend, it's okay to feel everything you're feeling. Even when you think you're supposed to be strong, it's okay not to be. It's okay to lean on someone else. It's okay to ask for help. It doesn't mean you are weak; asking for help *makes* you strong. Give yourself time, allow yourself to let go of everything you've been holding in because I promise allowing yourself to be vulnerable only makes you stronger.

Human

Sometimes we forget that we are only human— we go through ups and downs, twists and turns. Life is unpredictable, fragile, and constantly changing. There are bound to be unexpected surprises and bumps along the way. So let your river of emotion flow and allow yourself to feel its depth. Be kind to yourself as you go about your day. Stay proud of yourself even when you make mistakes because you're trying; you're growing. Keep your head held high even when you want to tuck it under the covers. Nobody said this journey would be free of bumps and bruises. Nobody said it would all be smooth sailing. Beautiful friend, you are human. Allow yourself to be.

Taking care of yourself means nourishing yourself within
to be able to take on the world out there.

Care

You've got to take care of yourself. And not just once in a while or only when you realize how desperately you need it, but every single day. Truly taking care of yourself means nourishing your mind, body, and spirit in a way that works for *you*. It means finding a balance within your everyday life that allows you to do the things you love. Taking care of yourself means finding peace amidst the busy days. It means nourishing yourself from within to be able to take on the world out there.

This is your life to cheer for yourself,
to celebrate yourself, as you go and as you grow.

Expectations

Let go of other's expectations for your life and start creating your own. Create your own expectations for the home you want to live in. Create your own expectations for the job you want to give your time and energy. Know that only you get to decide what goals you want to chase and what ideas you want to make come alive. You get to decide the clothes you wear and the meals you enjoy. You get to decide *everything*. Others may have opinions for you and your life, but at the end of the day, no one else can walk your path for you. Beautiful friend, your life is up to you.

Different paths

Every single person you have ever met and every person you will ever meet is a work in progress. So when you find yourself comparing yourself to others, remember that you're on your own unique path. And that means that your life won't look exactly like anyone else's and that that's okay; that's how it's *supposed* to be. Learn from others and get inspired by them, but never let yourself think *you* should be any different. Don't let yourself think you should be further along or better than where you are right now. Find it in your heart to love the unique path you're on, including the place you're in right now. Find it in your heart to celebrate your big and little wins, regardless of what they might mean to others because they're important to your path. Beautiful friend, this is your life to cheer for yourself, to celebrate yourself as you go and as you grow. Others may seem like beautiful, twinkling stars in the night, but you too are a shining sun.

No limits

Never let others limit your dreams. We are born from impossible odds into an impossible world. The chance of us being here right now is basically zero. So when someone has limited views of the world, don't take it to heart. Don't let their views bring yours down. Dream really big. Follow your vision and see where it takes you. Do the things others aren't willing to do. When it comes down to it, we are only here a little while to turn the impossible into possible. So why *not* go for it?

Decide

Let go of the expectations that are weighing you down. Let go of the pressures given by others to be a certain way, to have a certain job, to have a certain home, to act a certain way. Remind yourself that you don't need to have your life figured out by twenty-two or even by sixty-two. Know that you don't need to make some amount of money or have a certain amount of kids. You don't need to wear that brand or watch that show or spend Saturdays a certain way. You're allowed to make your own decisions about your life, regardless of what others may think. You get to decide what you should and shouldn't do. You get to decide what things make sense for you and your life and what things don't. So decide. Decide to set down others' opinions and form your own. Decide to make your life entirely up to you.

Grow Your Fire

When you open yourself up to the world,
it opens itself up to you.

Soulful

Do more of the things that inspire you. Listen to your favorite music more often. Make more of your own art, your own music. Try something new every now and again. Keep it fresh. Start keeping a journal. Start doodling on post-its and hang them around your home. Do the things you've been wanting and meaning to do for *so* long. Play the games you love. Watch the movies you laugh at every time you see them. Nourish your creative side. Nourish the child inside of you that is curious, that finds boundless joy in the little things. Beautiful friend, take time to nourish your soul.

Truth

Take the time to get to know yourself. Where do you come from? Who do you care about the most? What makes your soul sing? What brings you down? When do you feel the most joy? How would you spend your time if there were no limitations? Ask yourself the big questions because the more you get to know all of the magical things that make you so wonderfully you, the more you'll find your true path, the more you'll feel at home in your own skin. Be vulnerable and gentle with yourself; allow yourself time and space to learn who you are and to create your vision of who you want to become.

Curiosities

Make the extra effort to try new things as often as you can. Try out painting or dancing. Try cooking something new. Try skiing down a mountain or swimming in the ocean. Try reading a new genre or signing up for a class to learn something new. Follow your curiosities for their own sake. Follow them simply because it's fun. Never be afraid to branch out into the unknown because it's in the unknown that you'll find infinite possibilities. And one just might change your entire life.

Adventurous

Open yourself up to the world. Take adventures in your own town. Visit the local shops you've never walked into before. Explore new places whenever you get the chance. Seek new perspectives of the world. Talk to people you might not normally talk to. Keep an open mind. Take more walks around your neighborhood. Climb more mountains. Keep a journal and write about your experiences. Take chances... Because when you open yourself up to the world, it opens itself up to you.

Making room

Sometimes you have to let go of the life you thought you wanted in order to make room for the life you're truly meant for. The things standing in your way might be there to steer you in another direction. The disappointments might be there to guide you towards trying something new. The wonderful surprises might be there to show you something you're meant to have more of... So when life takes you in an unexpected direction, keep your heart open and trust that it is taking you closer to where you're meant to be.

Nikki Banas

Don't wait to be kind, because you never know
who needs it the most.

Kindness

Kindness is one of the most forgotten, yet most wonderful gifts you can give. Kindness has the power to heal wounds and spread hope. It can brighten someone's day and turn around their entire week. It can remind someone how wonderful they are in case no one else has told them lately. Kindness can remind someone that they aren't ever alone, even if they feel like it sometimes. It can encourage someone to be themself, without hiding who they truly are. It brings us together and reminds us that we really are more similar than we are different.

Warmth

Sometimes it's easier to be cold and distant; it's easier to separate ourselves and feel like they're different than we are. It's *hard* to be vulnerable and warm. It's hard to get closer and let ourselves be seen as we are and see others as they are too. Choose warmth anyways. Choose to have an open mind anyways. Choose to try and understand anyways. Because at the end of the day, we're not all that different… We may have grown up in different places and environments, we may have different families and different dreams, but we're all just trying to do our best with what we've got.

Sometimes we forget the
power in saying just a few words:
I see you. I believe in you.
I'm rooting for you.

Forgive

Forgive. Find it in your heart to let go of your anger and disappointments. Don't think about getting even. Don't think about revenge. Don't hold onto bitterness or resentment because the longer you do, the deeper your cuts will become. Forgiveness doesn't mean that what they did was right or justified; it means that you will no longer punish yourself with sadness and pain for what they did. It means that you allow those moments to be part of your past, but that you'll no longer carry them into your future. Sometimes it might be hard to forgive, but it's much harder to hold onto the pain.

Encourager

Be an encourager. Be someone who builds others up. Be the person who says, *I believe in you, you got this*... Sometimes we forget the power in saying just a few words: *I see you. I believe in you. I'm rooting for you.* These words turn ambitions into fulfilling careers. They turn dreams into new world records, they turn ideas into thriving businesses...These words are the ones that change lives.

Spread kindness

Be kind. Spread the love you want to see in the world. Spread smiles to those around you. Be sincere in your compliments and give them more often. When someone is talking to you, really listen to what they're saying and how they're saying it. Give others your full attention when you're spending time with them. Be honest, no matter how difficult it may be. Take a few moments to help someone out. Check in with your friends often. Call your parents more. Write a handwritten letter and send it to someone you care about. Sometimes the world can feel cold, but that's even more reason to spread warmth.

Impact

You never really know the true impact you have on those around you. You never know how much someone needed that smile you gave them. You never know how much your kindness turned someone's life around. You never know how much someone needed that long hug or deep talk. So don't wait to be kind. Don't wait for someone else to be kind first. Don't wait for better circumstances or for someone to change. Just be kind, because you never know who needs it the most.

Love

When you find people who unconditionally take you as you are, hold onto them so very tight. They're the ones that don't mind if you're having a bad day; they'll stay with you anyways. They're the ones who care about how you are really feeling, even if you can't find the words within you. They're the people you can talk to without worrying about what they'll think; they take you as you are. Make sure that whenever you find people like this, you keep them close. And whenever you get the chance, be one of them too.

Vulnerability is required for starting
anything new because you are headed to a place
that you haven't been before.

Beginnings

You can start something new whenever you want. You can start running today or next week or next month. You can start that new project tomorrow or next year. You can start learning how to paint this afternoon or during your lunch break tomorrow. If there's something you've been wanting to do, regardless of what it is, know that you can start whenever you want. You can start when you feel ready or when you feel far from ready. You can start when you have a plan or when you only have an idea of the first step. You can start on Monday or at noon on Thursday. The truth is you really can start something new whenever you want. So if an idea or a goal has been floating in your head, beautiful friend, why not now?

Gentle

The beginning can be the hardest part. You might feel uncertain of what's going to happen. You might feel nervous about what the outcome will be. You might be overwhelmed at a long road ahead of you. You might not even know if you can do it. So be gentle with yourself. Be kind to yourself. Vulnerability is required for starting anything new because you're headed to a place that you haven't been before. There is no way to know everything that's going to happen, that's just the nature of doing something new. Remind yourself that every athlete was once unfamiliar with the gym. Every artist was once lost in all the possible colors and brushes. Every CEO didn't know where the restrooms were in the office at first. Every senior in college was once a freshman in high school too... So be gentle with yourself when you begin. Let yourself be new at something, allow yourself to be a beginner. You'll get where you want to go and you'll grow more than you can imagine, beautiful friend, but you'll only get there if you allow yourself to be a beginner first.

Today

Give it your best, today. Right here, right now. Whatever you're working on or working towards, give it every single ounce of strength and courage you have inside of you today because you can't use today's effort, tomorrow… You can't make up for today, tomorrow. The future is made of the same beautiful things as today. So do whatever you've been wanting to do. Start working on that idea you've been thinking about. Reach out to that friend you've been meaning to talk to… Whatever you've been hoping you'd have time for, do that today. Make the time. Don't wait any longer, beautiful friend. The future is wonderful for dreaming, but today is best for doing.

Knowing

You don't have to know what comes next. You don't have to have everything figured out right this second. You don't need to know your entire story. You are a living, changing, growing soul riding through your unique and beautiful journey of life. And that's exactly what it is— a journey— and it wouldn't be a journey if you knew everything that was coming next. It wouldn't be a journey if you knew how it would all turn out in the end. So be patient with yourself and smile at not knowing, because your story is just starting to be written.

When you take just one little step each day,
eventually you'll find that all of those
little steps together conquered mountains.

Growth

Your growth is your own. Who you become, who you decide to grow into and what you choose to do is entirely up to you. No one else can walk your path; no one else can decide what's right or wrong for you. There is no finish line; there is no competition at all. Your growth is your own. So grow in the ways that *you* want to grow. Work on becoming your own best self, regardless of what others are doing. Push yourself closer to your dreams. Strive to get just a little bit better with each new day. When you take just one little step each day, eventually you'll find that all of those little steps together conquered mountains.

Environment

A cactus won't grow in a rainforest and a sunflower won't grow in a snowy tundra. A penguin can't thrive in a warm savanna and a tiger can't survive in a barren desert. And sometimes we forget that people are like that too. Sometimes you can be doing everything right, but your environment is simply not suited for your growth. Others may be dragging you down. You may not have enough time to do what you need to do because your calendar is already full... Our environments shape our growth. Who we spend time with affects who we become. You might need a lot of quiet time to yourself or many hours with close friends. You might need tough love or you might thrive off of gentle encouragement. You might need to write in a journal or have someone to talk with each day. No matter what things you need, *find them*. Find what helps you grow. Find the people who help you become your best self. Find the places you feel most inspired. Hold onto these people and places beautiful friend, and allow yourself to *bloom*.

Play your cards

You are the only one in charge of your life.
Unfair things will happen to you, unfortunate times may
come to you, but you get to choose how you respond. You
can choose whether you'll stay down or stand back up. You
can choose to let hard times break you or you can choose
to keep fighting strong. When unkind things happen to
you, you can choose to live in frustration and bitterness, or
you can find it in your heart to be the bigger person. In this
world, not a single person chooses the cards they receive,
but every single person chooses how they play theirs.

One day at a time, little by little,
you will get where you are meant to go.

Limitless

The only way to know your limits is to test them. And the only way to test your limits is by pushing yourself as close as you possibly can to what you *think* you are capable of. More often than not, you'll find that your limits were never real. You'll find that you can soar right past them and that you can run farther, connect deeper and learn more than you ever thought possible. You might even find yourself wondering why you had those false limits in the first place... So chase your limits. Don't be afraid to see how close you can get. Learn what you are really capable of because once you do, your world just might become limitless.

You've come so far

One day at a time, little by little, you will get where you are meant to go. Sometimes you don't realize how far you've come until you take a look back and see how much you've grown, how much you've changed already. Remind yourself of where you were a year ago, even a month ago. Remind yourself of how different things are now and the ways you've changed. Look at everything you've learned. Think about the things that you fought so hard to overcome. Remember the times that you thought you'd never be able to do it, but then you did. Remind yourself of the mountains you've conquered. Think of all the amazing things you've done already... You may not feel like you are growing right now, but *you are*. You are transforming, you are becoming even more you, you are getting ready for something so big and so incredible that's coming... And someday, not too far away, you will look back on right now and smile at how far you've come.

Transformation

Growing and changing aren't always easy, beautiful friend; transformation never is… There are going to be moments that break your heart. There will be days when you reach your breaking point. There will be times when you just can't hold on any longer… But do it. Hold on just a little longer. Know that you are in the process of becoming. Trust that you are changing and growing and becoming so much stronger. Know that you are transforming from the inside out into who you're meant to become. It might take time, but it will be worth it. *It always is.*

New light

Stars are born from chaos. They are born only after they first collapse. So beautiful friend, when you find yourself collapsing, when you find yourself lost in the midst of chaos and confusion, know that it's because a new beginning is coming. Know that everything is spinning and turning inside of you in order to form new worlds that you can't even imagine yet. Everything is quietly working under the surface to bring a new light— and it will shine brighter than ever.

Set down your troubles, your doubts, and your heartaches from today. Don't let them carry into tomorrow. They serve no purpose there.

Healing

Your wounds will heal because that's what wounds are meant to do. Your cuts and scrapes may leave behind scars; they may take longer to heal than you hope; they might bruise first before healing. And it's the same when it comes to matters of the heart. When you find yourself heartbroken or disappointed, broken or shattered, know that you *will* heal. The pain might bring you to your knees right now. The bruises may ache with even the smallest touch. The hurt might make you sick to your stomach and bring tears to your eyes. But beautiful friend, your heart too, will heal. Give yourself time. Give yourself kindness and warmth. Soon, you will heal and become stronger than you ever were before.

Making room

It's not about simply forgetting and moving on; that's never how it works. That's not how grief works. That's not how sadness works. That's not how disappointment works... You've got to make a little home inside of you for those memories and feelings. Whether you want them there or not, those memories are a part of you now. Your happy memories will stay with you— but so will your sad ones. So you have to make room. You have to allow yourself to feel them all deeply and accept that they are a piece of you. You will never be able to force out their intensity, their depth, their persistence. So let them in instead. Be vulnerable with yourself and allow yourself to feel every raw emotion entirely. Feel them and accept them, and know that even though they are a part of your yesterdays, they do not get to define your tomorrow.

Stand back up

When life knocks you down, stand back up as soon as you can. Because the longer you stay down, the harder it will be to get back up again. Do something that lifts your spirits. Talk to a friend that always makes you laugh. Take a walk outside and breathe in the fresh air. Whatever you do, keep your shoulders back, your head held high, and stand back up again. Don't stay down and wish things were better. Go out there and start making them better.

New day

Once the day comes to a close, let it remain closed. You did your best with everything that came your way today. Even if you made mistakes, had some trouble, or struggled to balance everything into one little day, let the page turn into tomorrow. It's okay if everything didn't go as planned— things don't always do. So set down your troubles, your doubts, and your heartaches from today. Don't let them carry into tomorrow because they serve no purpose there. Let them go and try your best tomorrow.

Moving forward

The life in front of you is so much more important than the life behind you. Don't let the heartbreaks and hurts keep you from becoming all that you are meant to become. No matter how difficult things were, *you made it through*. You are here now, and right now is a brand new opportunity for so many wonderful possibilities. Right now is an opportunity for a new beginning, for a new chapter to start. So make this chapter about hope, make it about overcoming. Make it the best one yet.

Waves

When tough times come your way, you really only have two options. You can either fight the waves or you can ride them. You can spend all your energy wishing things were different and wishing that situations and people would change. You can spend your precious time fighting against reality and all that is— or you can let go and ride the waves. You can soften. You can accept that life brings waves, and some waves will be undoubtedly wonderful but others will be incredibly tough. Beautiful friend, I hope you learn to ride your waves.

Growth takes time

Everything will work out exactly how and when it is supposed to, regardless of how and when you may want it to. Let your faith in your journey be stronger than your doubts and fears. Be patient with yourself and your growth, knowing that good things always take time. Give yourself time and space to try new things and explore different paths. Remember that growth never happens in a perfectly straight line. Setbacks and interruptions happen, and that's okay. Because in time, you will get where you are meant to go.

Shine from Within

Everything you need to bloom is
already inside of you.

Bloom

Bloom where you are. Bloom despite the weeds and grow tall and beautiful anyways. Bloom where you are even if you wish you were elsewhere. Take in all of the light when the sun is shining and know that the rain is necessary when it's not. Know that everything you need to bloom is already inside of you— you already have the strength and capability to grow. Nourish your body and take care of your mind. Keep learning and growing. Let your true colors shine. *Bloom.*

Lighter

When you fill your mind with thoughts of kindness, of love, faith, hope, joy, your life becomes those things. You start to see more kindness in the world. You start to feel more love as you go through your days. You start to notice yourself smiling more and more. You laugh easier and feel lighter. You start to feel more hopeful, more peaceful. Look for the light even when it's difficult to find. Search for the flicker of light even when it's dark because there is always more light to be found.

Write the story you'll want to reread
over and over again.

Your story

Write your story. Whenever you need, close the pages and start a new chapter. Scratch out the things that don't belong. Add in more of the things that bring you joy. Dream of your future and start writing the adventure towards it. Find the people that are meant to help you on your journey, and that you're meant to help on their journey too. Embrace the middle chapters when you're unsure of what's to come and you aren't yet at a climax because those middle parts are full of excitement and possibility too. Write your story because you are the only one who can. Write it with passion, write it with love… Most of all, write the story you'll want to reread over and over again.

No one else

The best way to be is to be yourself. It's to follow your heart even when you have doubts. It's to listen to your gut even when others disagree or don't think you can. It's to be silly and weird even when others don't understand. Being yourself is meeting yourself in your own skin and saying, *This is who I am.* It's about staying true to who you are and following your heart over anything or anyone else. It's about finding peace within your own skin and love within your own soul. It's about letting your own authentic self shine.

Stand out

It's okay to be different. It's okay to *not* follow the crowd. It's okay to be weird. It's okay to make your own path. And it's okay to see the world differently. The worst thing you could possibly do is pretend to be someone you're not, just to squish yourself into someone else's standards. Beautiful friend, make your own standards. Be bravely yourself. Stand out. Walk in the other direction. Be yourself no matter what, and the rest will work itself out.

Echo

I hope you never play small. I hope you never have to shrink yourself down or soften your sound simply to fit into the hum of the world. I hope your wildest dreams don't scare you and that you are never afraid to let your sound be heard. I hope you fail and mess up sometimes, because that means you're trying new things and going for bigger dreams... And most of all, I hope you never let those moments stop you from chasing. Because if you keep climbing, if you keep going big anyways, if you keep squeezing out every drop of effort you possibly can, beautiful friend, know that your divine melody will echo across the seas and stars endlessly.

Up to you

No one gets to decide who you are except for you. Period. No one gets to tell you how capable you are or who you can become. People will undoubtedly talk and give their opinions like they know something you don't. And people will not believe in you simply because they view the world from a lens of impossible. But you get to decide who to believe. You can believe the discouraging teacher and pessimistic friend, or you can believe the voice inside of you that knows you are made for more.

If something seems impossible but your
heart whispers go for it, beautiful friend,
go for it.

Compass

Let your heart be your compass through the winding roads and twists and turns of life. Whenever you come to a new crossroads, quiet down the outer world to listen to what your heart is saying. If something doesn't feel right, it probably isn't right. If your heart is saying not to do something, *that* is a reason not to do it. If something seems impossible but your heart says to go for it, *go for it*. You may not always know what your heart is pointing you towards, but it is always guiding you in the right direction.

Your heart knows

Be bold enough to listen to your heart, and more so, to follow it. Your heart has always known exactly who you are, what you are made of, and what you are made for. Your heart has always known that you are meant for a life of so much joy and love. Your heart knows you are meant for a life of living free.

Your heart speaks to you through your
feelings deep within while fear speaks through
others and judgments *out there*.

Heart

I think that life really comes down to deciding to follow your heart over your fears. Your heart speaks to you through your feelings deep within while fear speaks through others and judgments *out there*. Your heart can say to leave a relationship— but fear can say you'll be judged harshly for leaving. Your heart may say to start a new career— but fear may say you are comfortable where you are now and it's not worth the risk. If you follow your heart anyways, your life will undoubtedly change. You will be guided by your true self instead of fear or doubt. You will find the people and jobs and places *truly* meant for you, and the rest will fall into place.

Creating joy

If you trust your heart and follow your path wherever it takes you, you will find your greatest joys in life. And I think that that's what it's all about: finding your joys. It's about trying new things that interest you and trusting your heart about people and places and jobs and hobbies. It's about believing in yourself and doing what you love regardless of the outcome. It's about doing the things you want to do without fear or judgment. It's about finding joy. And when it's hard to find it, well… It's about creating joy where you are.

When you choose bravery, you are choosing to live despite your fears— not because of them.

Possible

Before anything else, you have to believe that it's possible. Even if there isn't much evidence of it working out. Even if no one else believes in you. Even if it's never been done before. You have to believe in yourself wholeheartedly because if you don't, who will? Belief alone won't get you there, but without it, you will *never* get there. You have to believe that it's possible, and you have to believe that it's worth fighting for.

Resilience

You never know when you are minutes away from a breakthrough. You never know when you are one project away from the promotion. You never know when you are one hour of studying away from passing the exam. You never know when you are one song away from landing the record deal. *That* is why you keep going, that is why you keep trying. That is why when you fall down, you stand back up. You stand back up because you have to give yourself a real chance. It might not happen fast, it might not happen how you thought, but that doesn't mean you should quit. All good things take time, and your time will come too.

Impossible

What if the impossible suddenly became possible for you? How would your life change? What would you do differently? Sometimes we forget that limitations come from our mind; not so much our reality. Flying across the globe was impossible, until someone made it possible. Running a four minute mile was impossible, until someone made it possible. Talking and seeing your loved one thousands of miles away was impossible, until someone made it possible... The thing about impossibilities is that the only way to prove that they are impossible is by trying. And often times in trying them, we find that they were actually possible all along.

Failures

Believe in yourself enough to not let failures stop you. Believe in yourself enough to let obstacles strengthen you. Beautiful friend, you are capable of doing anything you dream of doing. Period. You are capable of becoming who you want to become and you need to believe that with your entire being. It's okay if you make mistakes, it's okay if you fail one hundred times before you get it right. Life isn't about getting everything right on the first try. It's about standing up when you don't.

Bravery

Don't let the fear of being bad keep you from ever becoming good. Don't let the doubt keep you from ever trying. Be brave enough to start. Be brave enough to keep going. Be brave enough to be a beginner. Because no matter how it works out in the end, you gave your best. And when you try, when you give your best, when you choose bravery, you are choosing to live despite your fears— not because of them.

Becoming

Start removing your fears and doubts one by one and replacing them with kindness and courage instead. Start taking each doubt and responding to it with bravery. Answer each, *I could never do that*, with, *maybe I could try*. Turn every, *I'm just not like them*, into, *I can become whoever I want to become*. It's time to face your fears with courage because they serve no other purpose than to hold you back and keep you from becoming who you are meant to become.

I believe in me

You can do anything in this life if you truly believe that you can. It may be incredibly difficult and there may be many roadblocks and setbacks along the way. It could take longer than you want it to and it could be a harder climb than you ever thought possible... But if you believe in yourself and your capabilities, and you give it everything you possibly can to make it happen, it will happen. And it all starts with you. It all starts with you saying to yourself, *I believe in me.*

Support

**I hope you become someone you can count
on.** I hope you become the person that believes in you one
hundred percent, even through the moments when all you
want to do is give up. I hope you become the person who
gives it everything you have, even when you think it won't
be enough. And I hope you become the person who cheers
for you even when you're down. It takes a lot of courage
and love to become that person, but once you do, you'll
move mountains. You'll find bravery in yourself that you
never knew you had. You'll do all of the things that you
were once afraid to do. Nothing will be able to stop you
anymore. Nobody will be able to stand in your way because
you won't depend on them or their opinions; you will
simply count on *you.*

Why not you?

I am one of those people who believes that anything is possible. If you are working as hard as you possibly can and you believe 110% that you will achieve your goal, I believe that you will achieve your goal. Because you are so much more capable than you can imagine. You have so much possibility inside of you that is just waiting to come into this world. You can overcome any obstacle. You are made of the same stuff as the people you look up to. You are brave and capable and strong and wonderful. You can learn anything with some time and effort. So honestly, why *not* you?

Focus on just the one little step in front of you.
The rest will come when it's time.

Hope

If you only carry one thing throughout your entire life, let it be hope. Let it be hope that better things are always ahead. Let it be hope that you can get through even the toughest of times. Let it be hope that you are stronger than any challenge that comes your way. Let it be hope that you are exactly where you are meant to be right now, and that you are on the path to where you are meant to be... Because during these times, hope will be the very thing that carries you through.

Climbing mountains

You only need to focus on one little step forward. You don't need to conquer the entire mountain right now. You don't have to have everything figured out today. The only possible way to climb a mountain is by climbing it one step at a time. Don't think about the peak, don't worry about what might come later. Instead, focus on just the one little step in front of you. The rest will come when it's time. For now, it's just one little step forward.

Create a life you love. And as often as you need— remake your life into one you love.

Morning coffee

Enjoy the first sip of your morning coffee, and the second and third and fourth. Find something to smile about on your commute, whether it's listening to your favorite radio station or singing to your favorite albums. Take a break during your day to walk outside and feel the sun on your skin. Don't wait until the weekend to spend time with those you love most. Life is just too short and fragile to not live a life of chasing joy each and every day.

For love

Make time for everything you love— the people, the places, the things. Give your loved one an extra kiss, chat with your friend on the phone for another hour. Go out of your way to help a neighbor. Be a tourist in your favorite city and explore it like you've never seen it before. Reread the books you love and re-watch the tv shows that make you laugh every time. Make time for everything and everyone you love because a life lived for love is always, *always* worth it.

Your quest

Your quest is for passion and love. You are meant to live a joyful, vibrant, deeply felt life. You are meant to live a life that you are excited to wake up to every single day, regardless of what day it is. You are meant to live with wild passion and bold courage. So whenever you need, let go of the people, places, hobbies, and things that don't light a fire inside of you. Hold on tight to the people, places, dreams and art that fill your soul with life. Add more of what you love and what you can't go a day without thinking about. Create a life you love. And as often as you need— remake your life into one you love.

Never settle

Don't ever settle. Not with love. Not with your job. Not with your city. Not with your home. Not with your happiness. If something doesn't feel right, don't let it continue for too long. If it doesn't feel right, let it go and leave it behind. Even without a logical reason, even without knowing what you'll do next, leave it behind because it just doesn't matter. If it's not meant for you, let it go because one day you'll thank yourself for never settling on your happiness. One day you'll realize that you were meant for so much more and that you only found it because you never settled.

Sometimes we forget that every step of the way is equally important, whether it's the first or last.

Acceptance

Love yourself through it all, beautiful friend. Be vulnerable enough to accept your flaws and know that they are what make you human, they are what make you real. Be confident enough to accept and cherish your strengths. Don't minimize or hide them; they are your beautiful gifts to share with the world. Love yourself enough to say: You know what? All of this is who I am, messiness and all. I make mistakes. I can be late sometimes. Sometimes I forget things. I take things to heart easily. But... I'm doing my best with what I've got. And I'm so proud of that. I'm so proud of *me*, and I'm so proud of who I'm becoming.

Proud

I'm so proud of you. I'm proud that you keep showing up every single day. I'm proud of all the tough decisions you had to make and that even though it was hard, you stood your ground anyways. I'm proud that you never gave up on yourself and kept fighting for everything you love. I'm proud that despite everything you've been through, you still wake up and find ways to smile every day. I'm proud that even though you've seen so much darkness, you always keep searching for the light. I'm proud of you and how far you've come, and I'm excited for everything that's coming next too. Beautiful friend, I hope you're proud of you too.

Getting here

Love yourself because you have gone through so much to get here. You've climbed many mountains and jumped over countless hurdles. You've faced a lot of darkness and fought through many battles. You may not be where you want to be yet, but you've come so far already, and that deserves your endless love.

With every step

You can love yourself exactly as you are now
while also wanting to grow and become more. You can be
proud of how far you've come while also wanting to push
yourself even further. You don't have to pick just one or
the other. Beautiful friend, you can love yourself every
single step of the way… You've got to celebrate both your
big and little wins because it really is about your journey;
it's about your journey of becoming. Sometimes we forget
that every step of the way is equally important, whether it's
the first or last. Without one of them, the journey would
be incomplete… So love yourself through it all, love
yourself every single step of the way.

Entirely

It might be hard to love yourself sometimes, but it is much harder to *not* love yourself. You have to stop putting yourself down and instead, start building yourself up. You have to become someone you love by standing up for yourself, taking care of yourself, *nourishing* yourself. You've got to start loving yourself, inside and out. You have entire galaxies spinning inside of you. You have ideas and experiences and dreams that no one else has nor will ever have. You are brave and capable and strong and wonderful in so many ways… And you've got to love all of you, beautiful friend. Your soul, your heart, your fingers and your toes. You have to become someone you love because you are with you until the very end. So treat yourself with kindness. Take care of yourself, emotionally and physically. Nourish your soul. Love yourself entirely.

Happy

At the end of the day, what really matters is that you are doing what makes you happy. It's about following your heart wherever it leads you and being yourself wherever you go. It's about loving and celebrating who you are so much that it just doesn't matter what anyone else thinks. And it's about celebrating others and who they are too. It's about encouraging others to be who they are because there is no competition or race. Your life is about creating your own happiness; your life is about letting yourself shine.

Acknowledgments

I am deeply thankful for all of those who made this book possible. Thank you from the bottom of my heart. I am only me because of *you*.

To Dennis, for believing in me and every dream of mine since the moment we met. When I first told you I wanted to be a writer, despite all of the circumstances, you believed in me with your whole heart. Thank you for all of your love and encouragement along the way, I truly wouldn't be me without *you*.

To my family, for the life you've given me and for your endless love, encouragement, and laughter. Thank you for teaching me how to make every day special and for cheering for me in everything I do.

To Samantha, Tracy, & Phoebe. We don't talk nearly at all as much as we should, but I'm so blessed to call you my beautiful friends. You truly inspire *me*.

To my beautiful Instagram and Pinterest community. Without all of your kindness, love, & support, this book would not exist.

To the talented and selfless photographers who donate their works using Unsplash.com. And especially to the following, whose works appear in this book: *Javier Allegue, Jenna Anderson, Darius Bashar, Eli DeFarla,*

Esther Driehaus, Devan Freeman, Yeol J Gonzalez, Lynn Jordan, Aljoscha Laschgari, Clarisse Meyer, Olia Nayda, Emma Peneder, Priscilla Du Preez, Dominic Sansotta, Anna Utochkina, Jared Weiss, Kevin Wolf, Remi Yuan.

Printed in Great Britain
by Amazon